# Tavistock Ontario and Area in Photos, Saving Our History One Photo at a Time

Photography
by Barbara Raué
2012

Series Name:
Cruising Ontario

Book 15: Tavistock and Area

Cover photo:   The Glass Swan,
current Italianate style since 1892

# Series Name: Cruising Ontario

Book 1:  London
Book 2:  Dundas
Book 3:  Hamilton
Book 4:  Oakville
Book 5:  Chesley
Book 6:  Stoney Creek
Book 7:  Waterdown
Book 8:  Owen Sound
Book 9: Mount Forest
Book 10:  Dundalk
Book 11: Burford and Area
Book 12: Waterford and Area
Book 13: Drumbo and Area
Book 14: Sheffield and Area
Book 15: Tavistock and Area

# Other Books by Barbara Raue

Coins and Gems

Arrows, Indians and Love

The Life and Times of Barbara
Volume 1: Inventions That Have Enhanced My Life
Volume 2: Entertainment That I Have Enjoyed
Volume 3: East Coast Trip 2009
Volume 4: Olympics
Volume 5: Wonders of the World

## Tavistock

Tavistock is located 15 kilometres southeast of Stratford and five kilometres south of Shakespeare on County Road 59. The world championship crokinole tournament has been held here annually since 1999. In 1848, Captain Henry Eckstein founded Tavistock.

## Baden

Castle Kilbride, built in 1887 by James Livingston, co-founder of a successful linseed oil company, is located in Baden. Baden was the home town of Sir Adam Beck, the pioneer of hydro-electric power. Baden is located on Snyders Road northeast of New Hamburg and west of Kitchener. The Baden Tower, a huge television, radio and communications tower, is located on top of one of the Baden Hills. From here CKCO-TV transmits its signal. Much of the area consists of farmlands and there are pine forests as well.

## New Hamburg

The Nith River winds through town and flows through the downtown core which is home to a 50 foot waterwheel built in 1990. New Hamburg is on Highway 7 about midway between Stratford to the west and Kitchener to the east. It was founded in the 1830s by a group of German settlers.

Tavistock

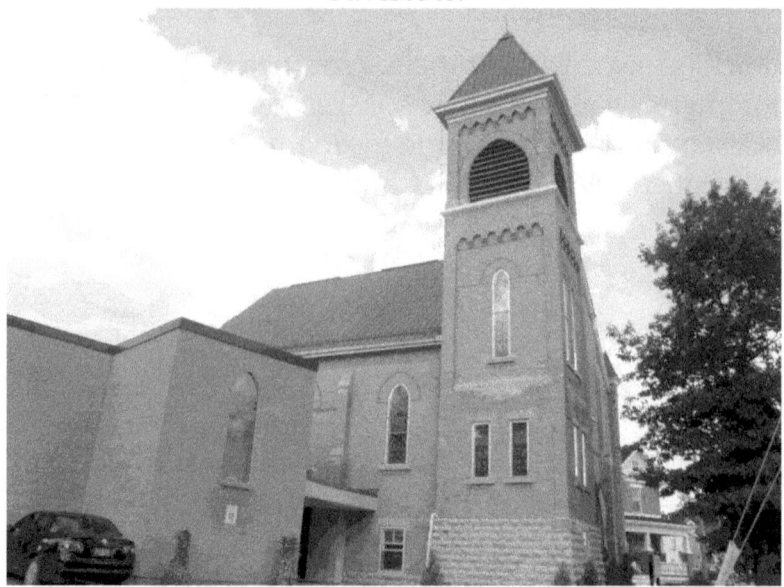

(Original name Zion Evangelical Church)
Grace United Church – built 1904

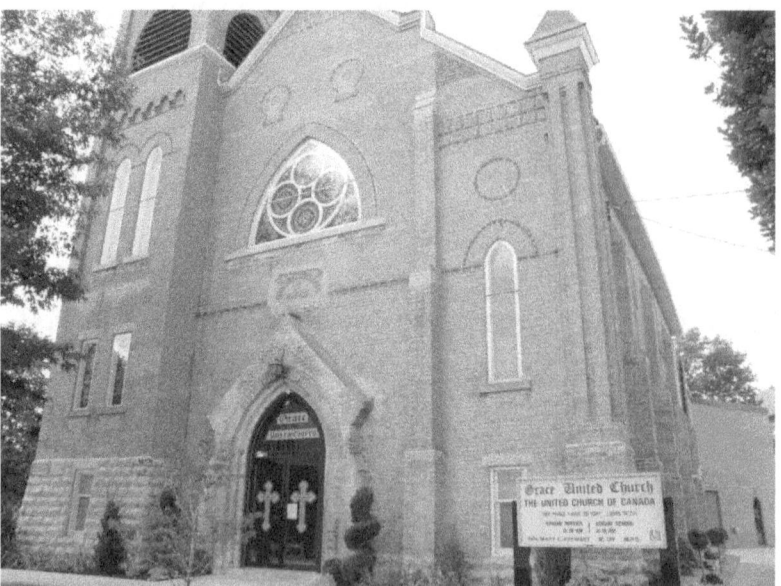

Beautiful rose window, fancy brickwork for decoration

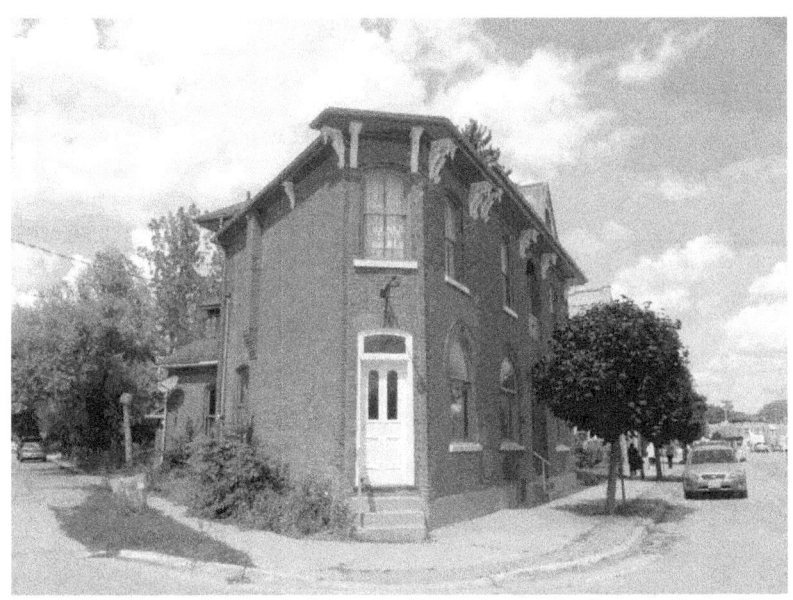

The Glass Swan – late Italianate style has existed
since 1892 when Dr. Otto Niemeier bricked over
two adjoining structures

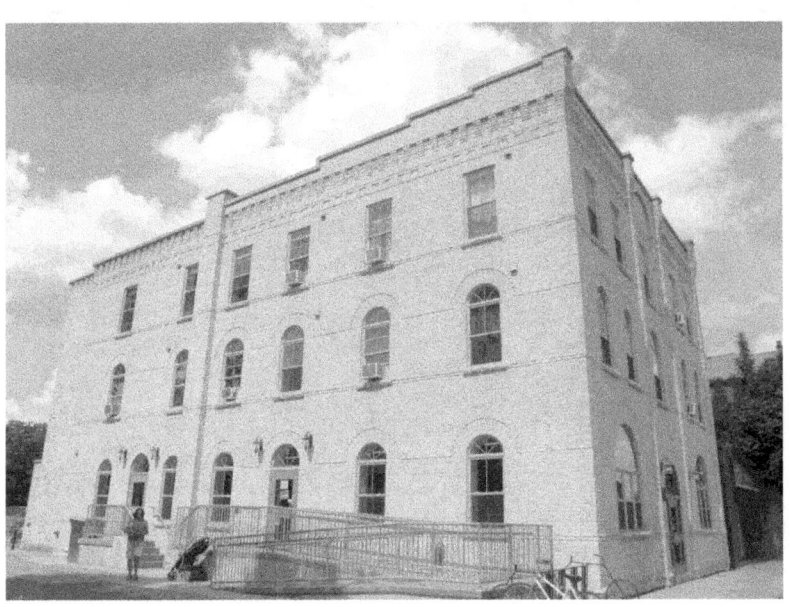

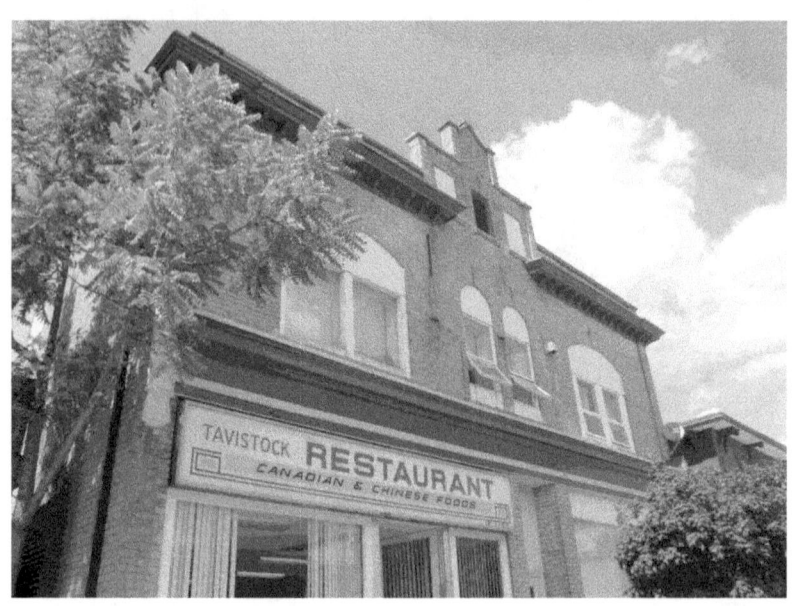

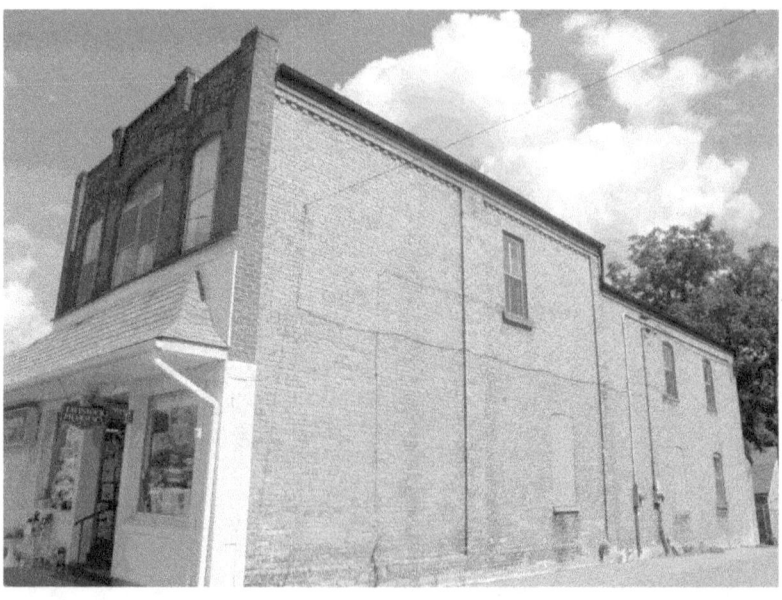

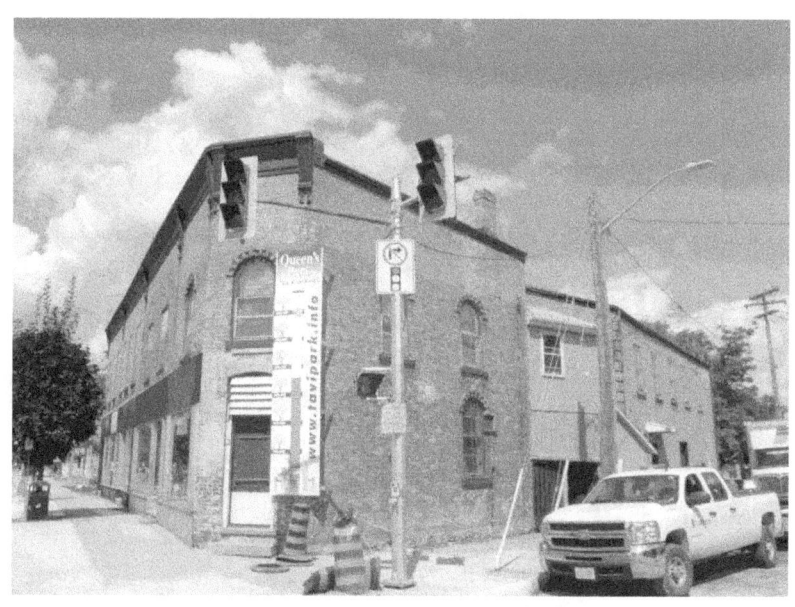

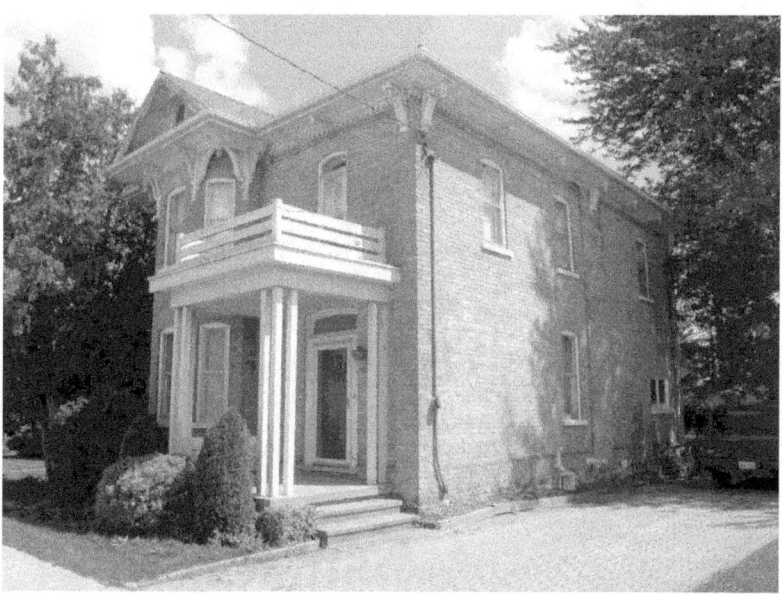

paired cornice brackets under the eaves

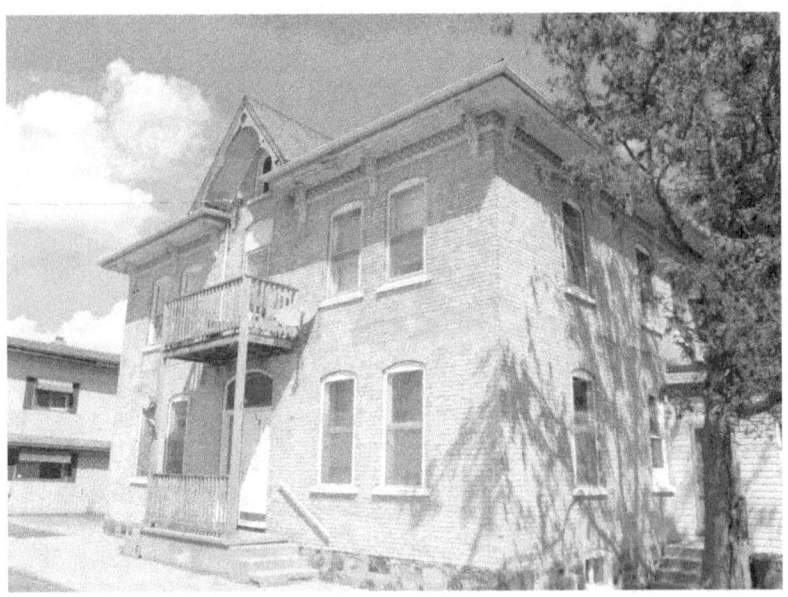

Single cornice brackets

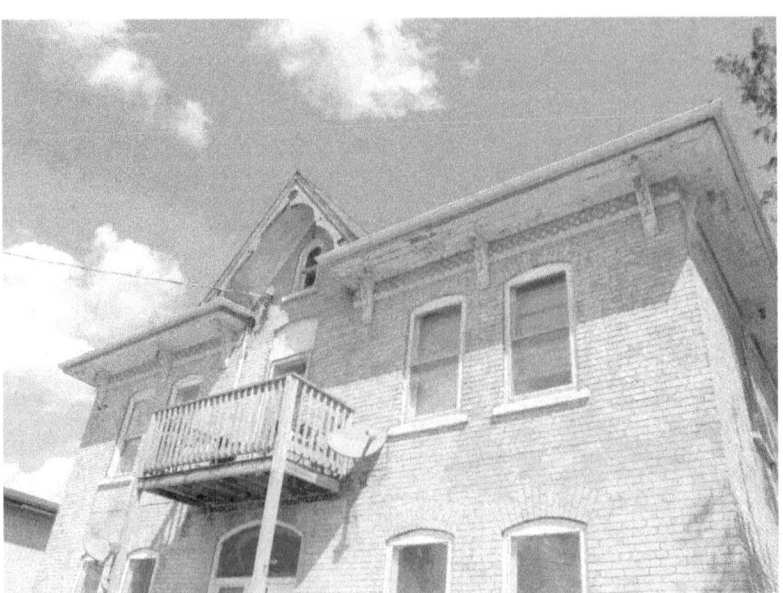

Gingerbread verge board around gable

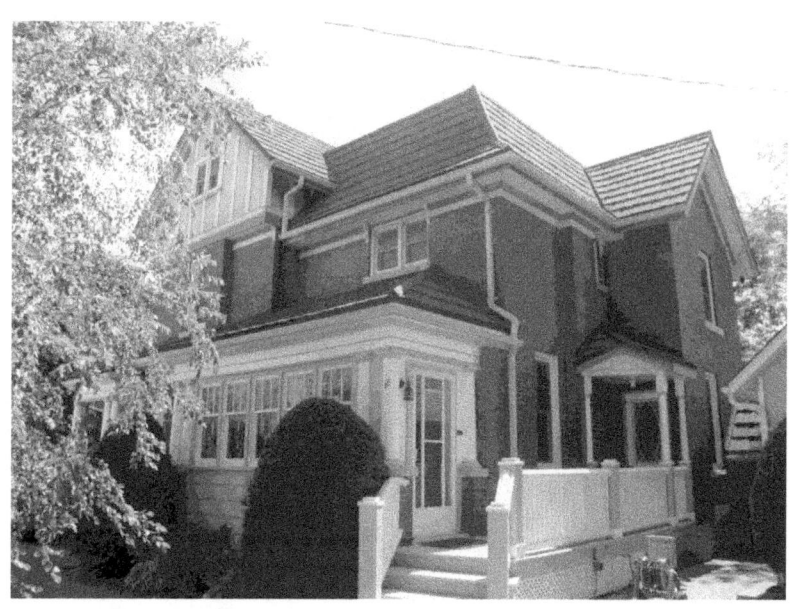

#18 – Italianate style

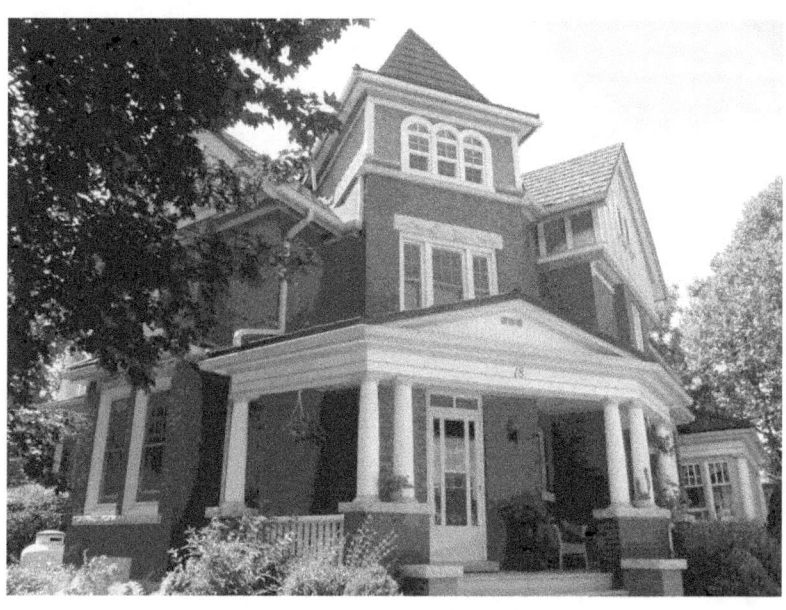

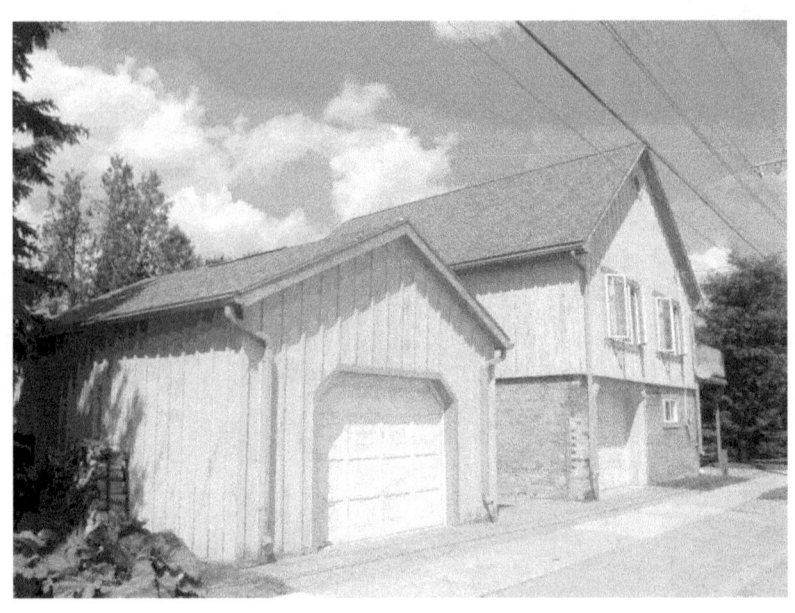

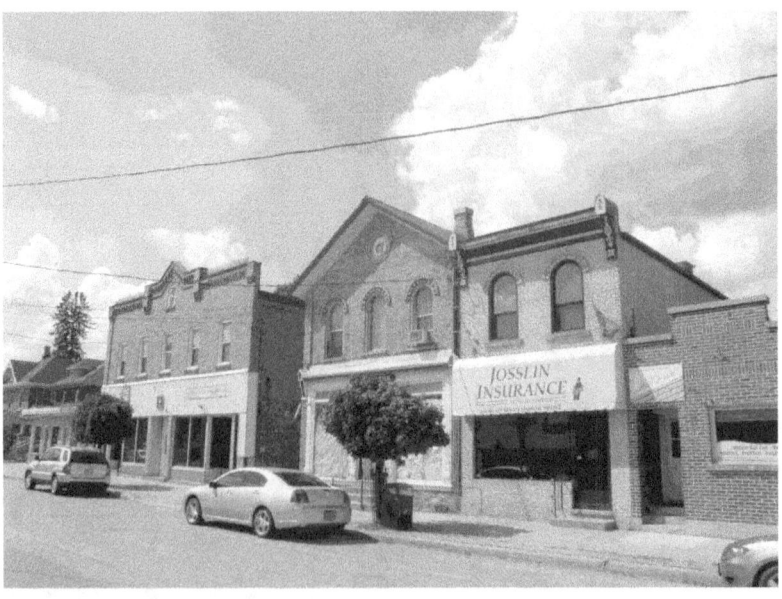

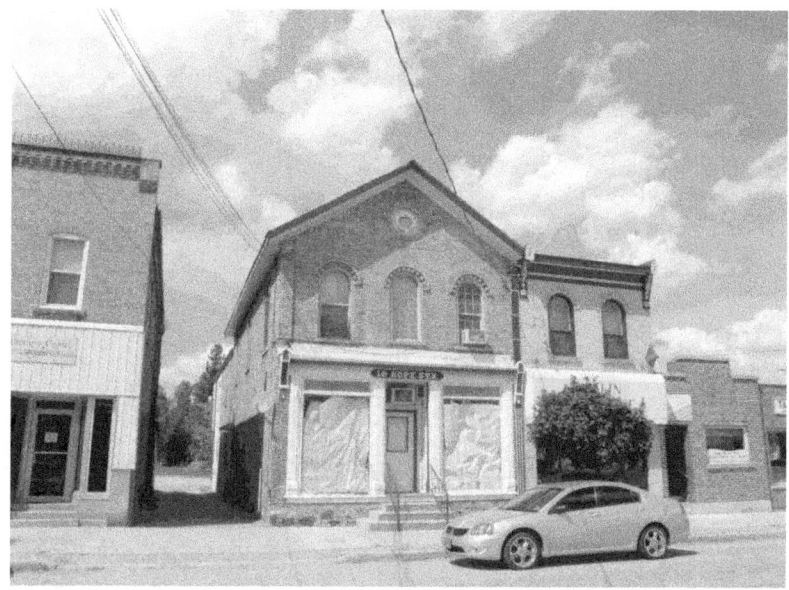

16 Hope Street West

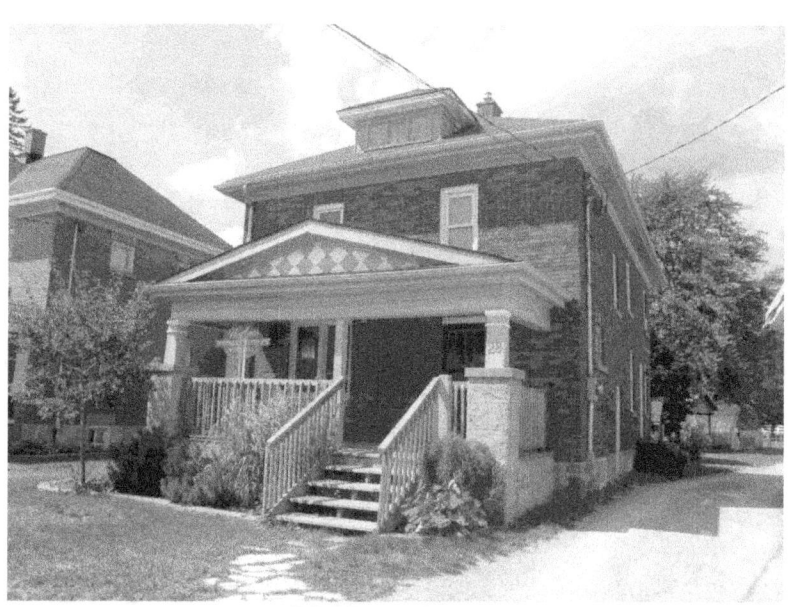

28 Hope Street

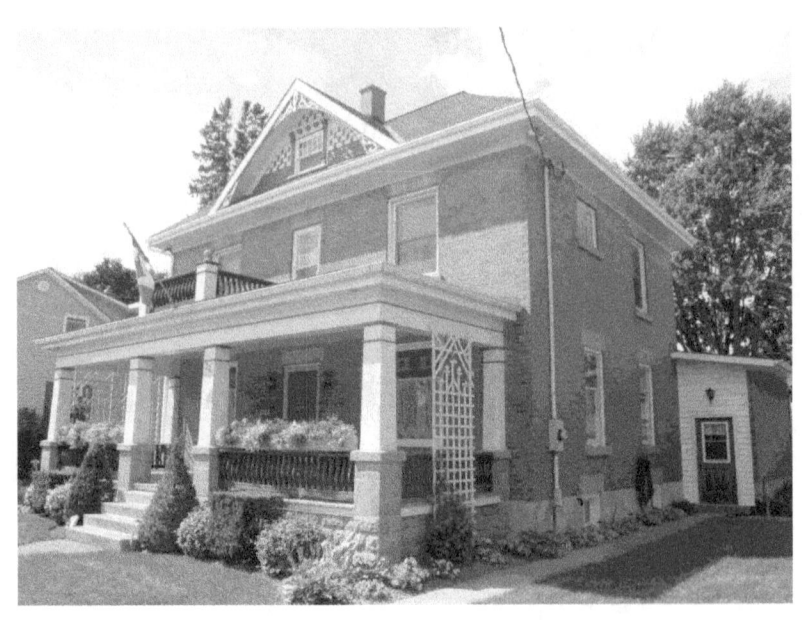

32 Hope Street

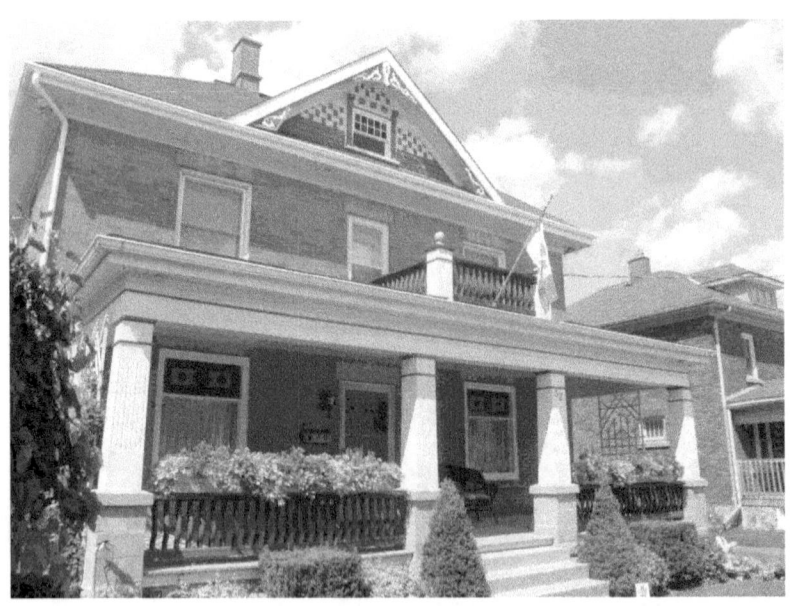

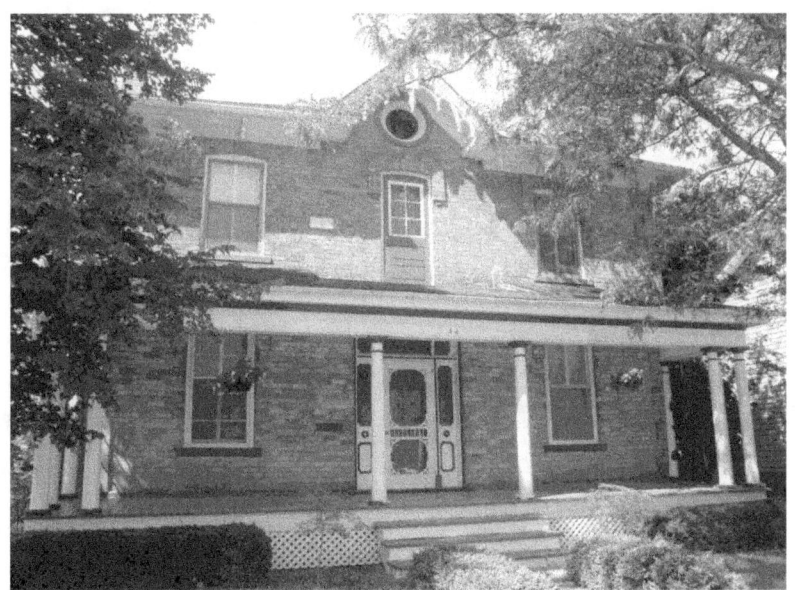

44 Hope Street

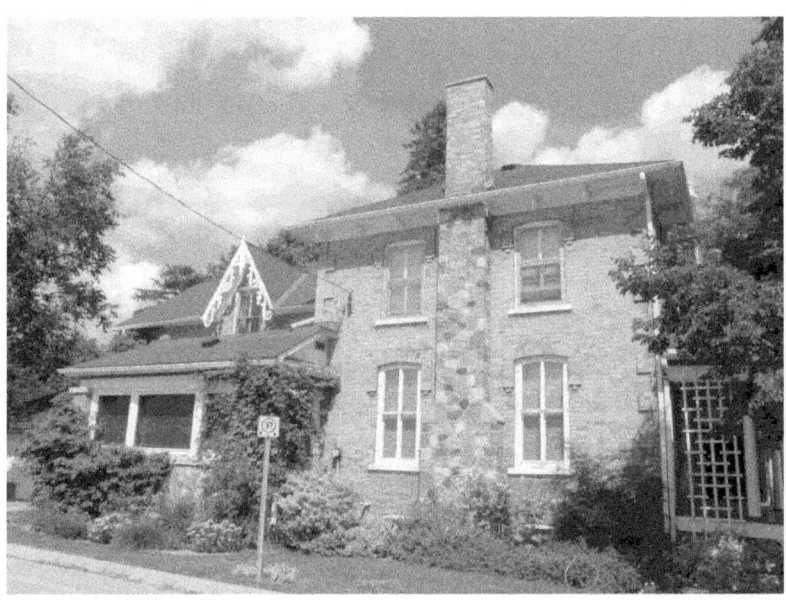

Yellow brick, two storey, verge board trim, stone chimney

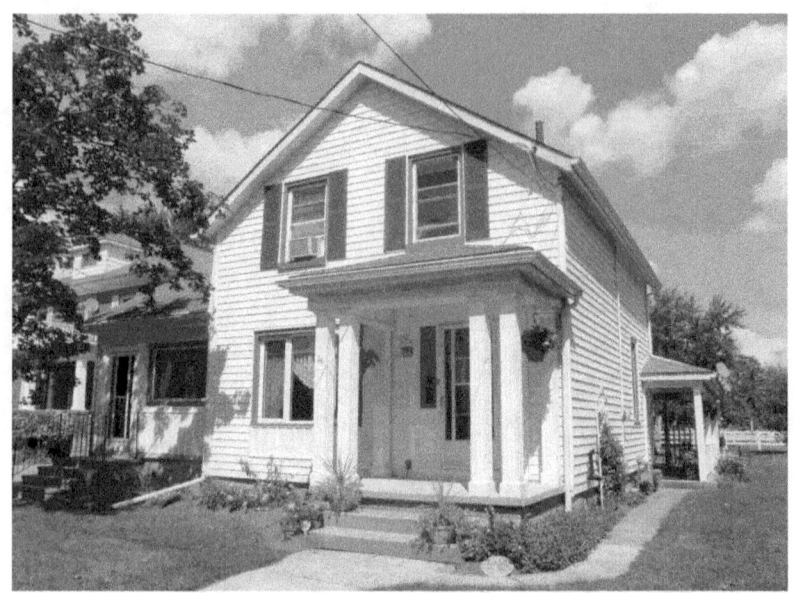

#24 – with Doric style columns

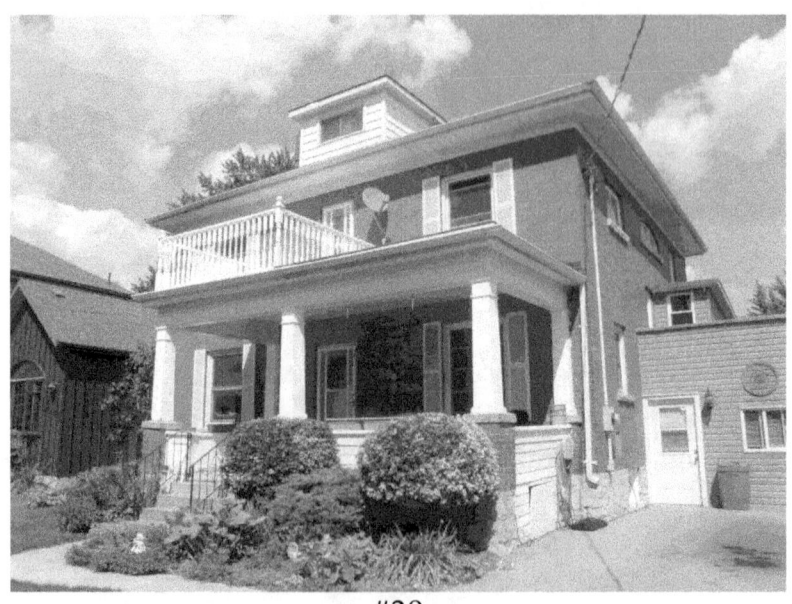

#30

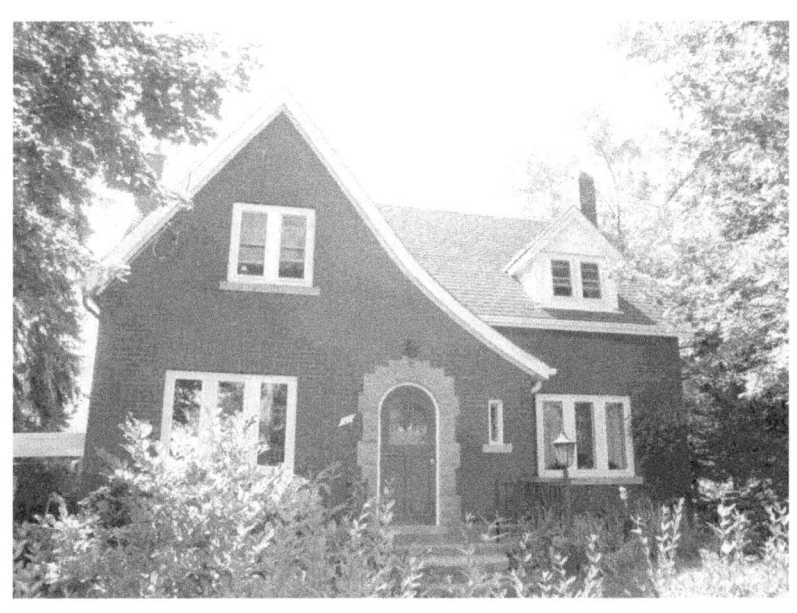

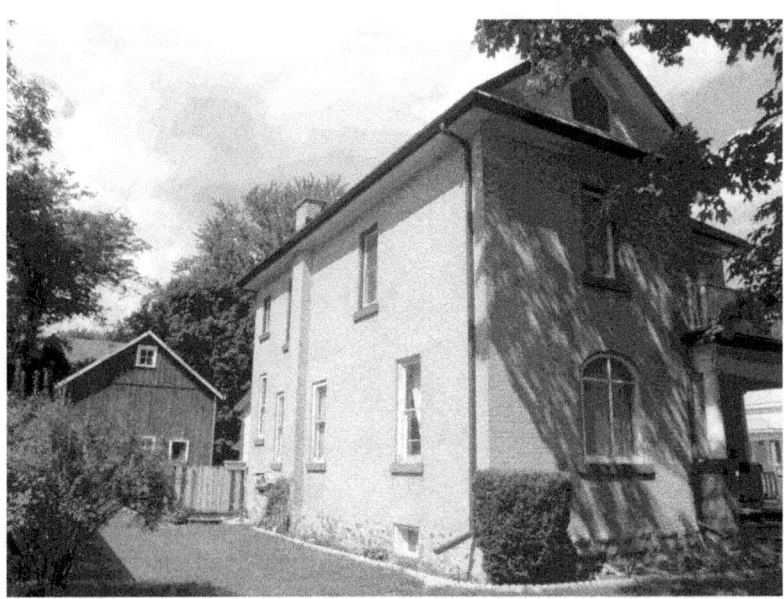

Stone basement

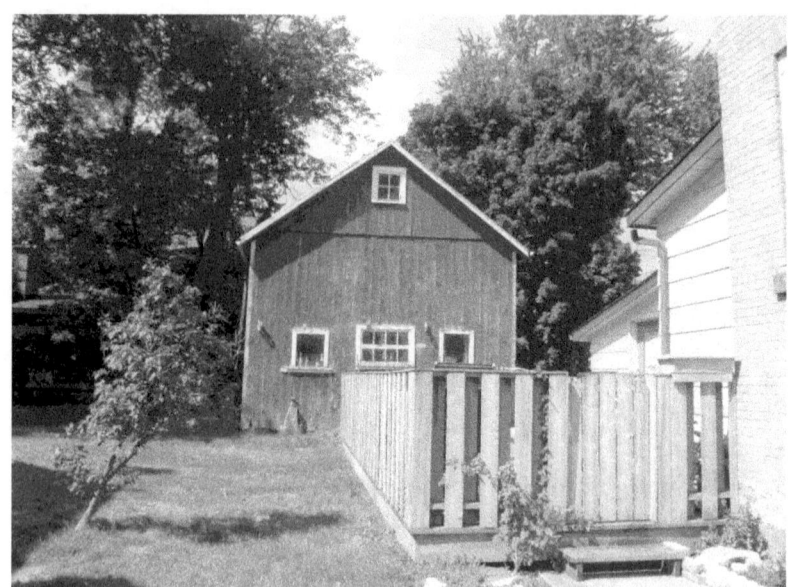

Old wooden shed

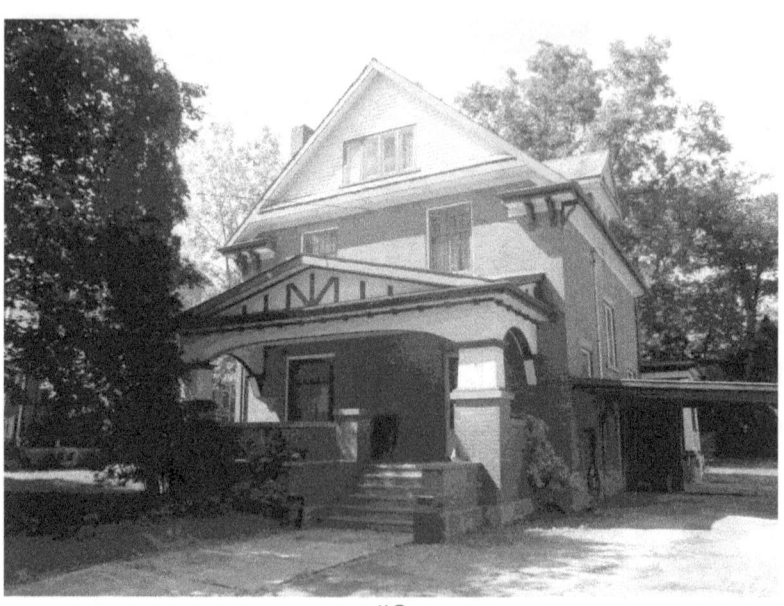

#8

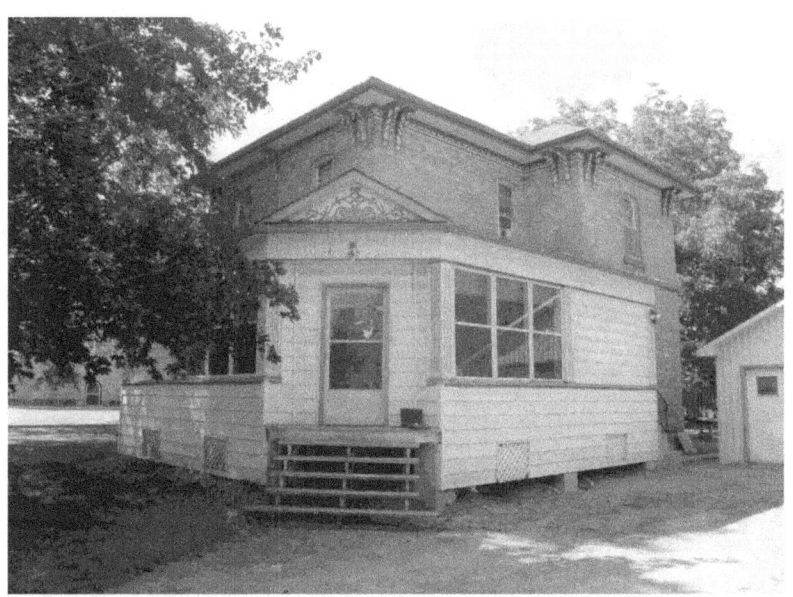

Paired cornice brackets and fancy work in the gable

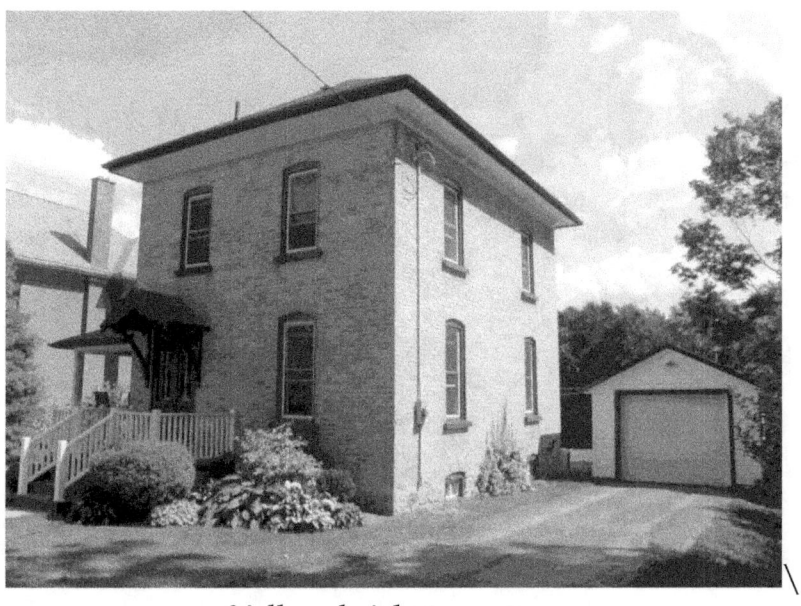

Yellow brick, two storey

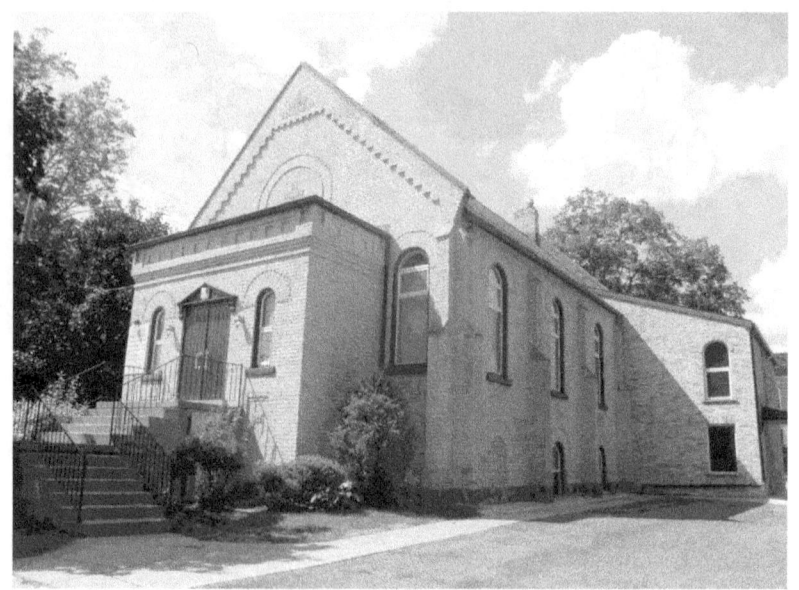

Tavistock Bible Chapel – 32 Oxford Street

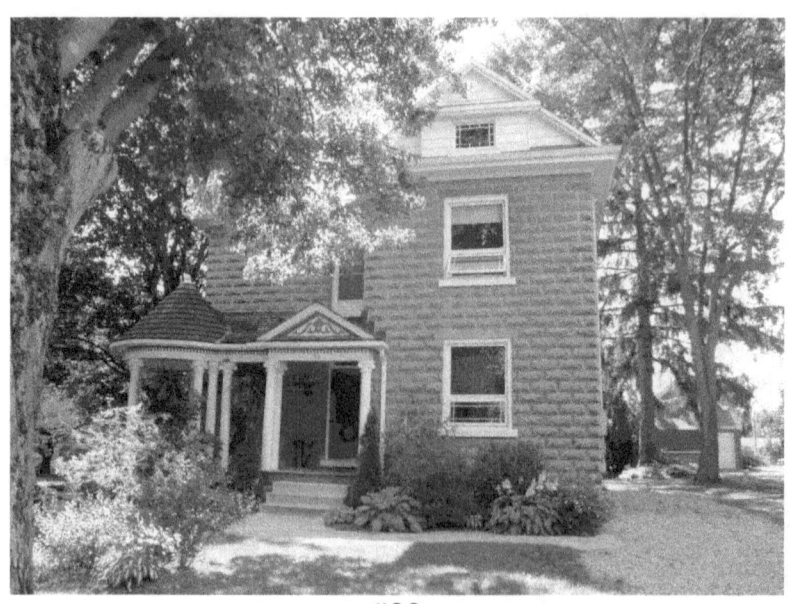

#39

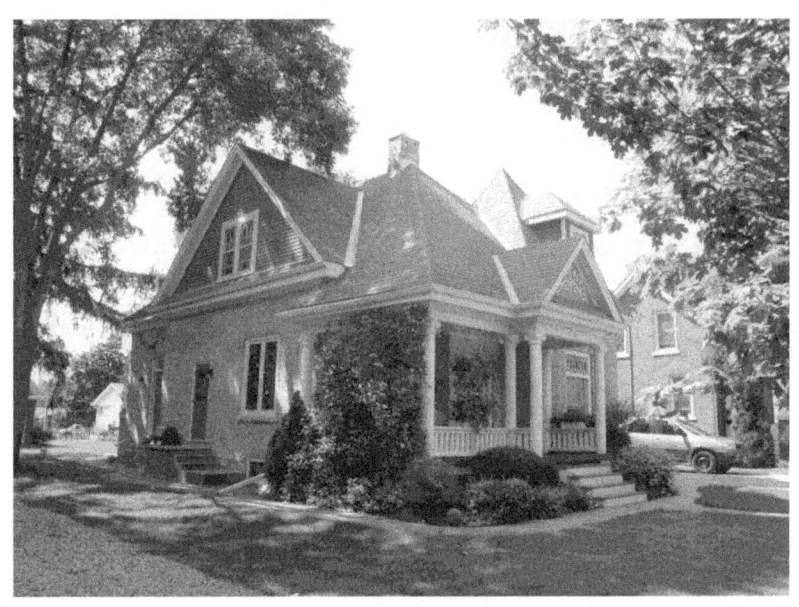

# 45 – Hillcroft

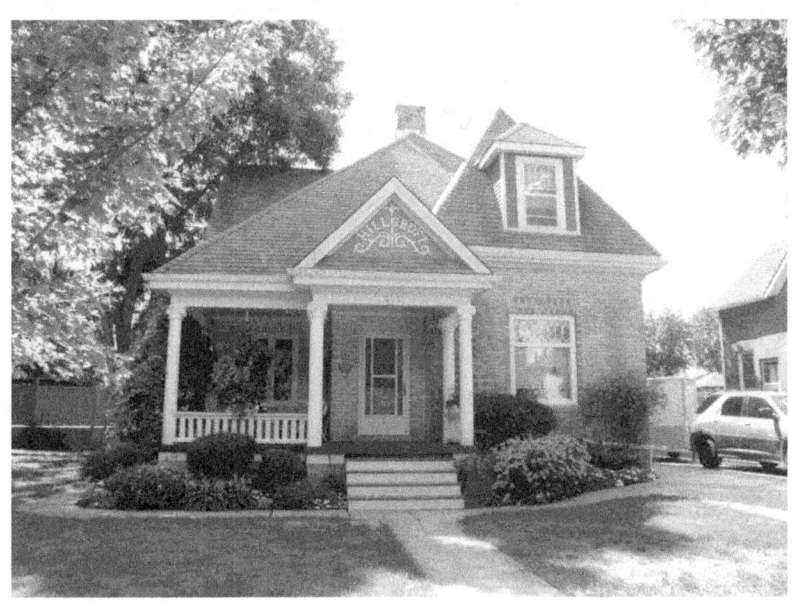

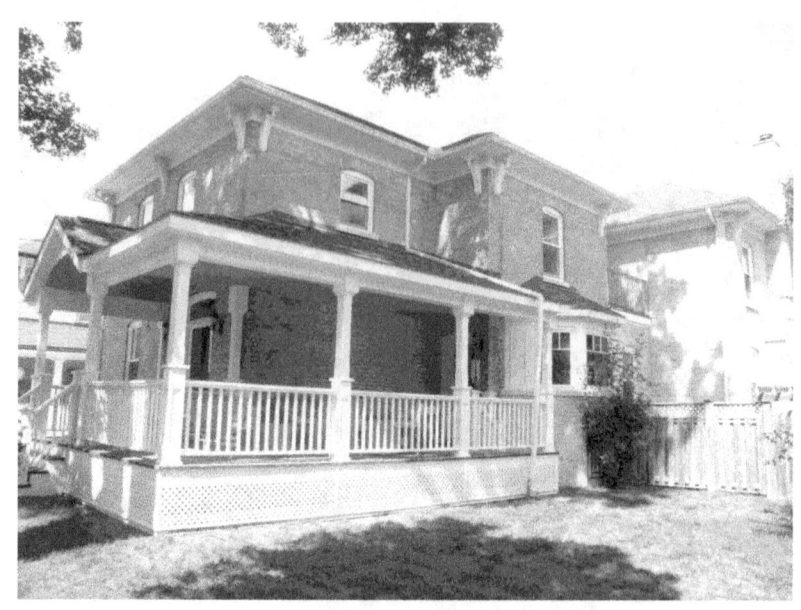

#54

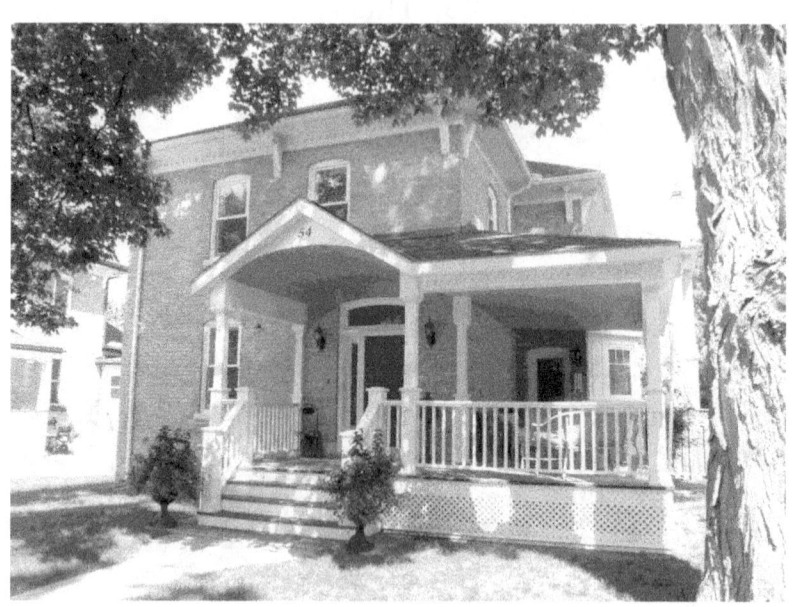

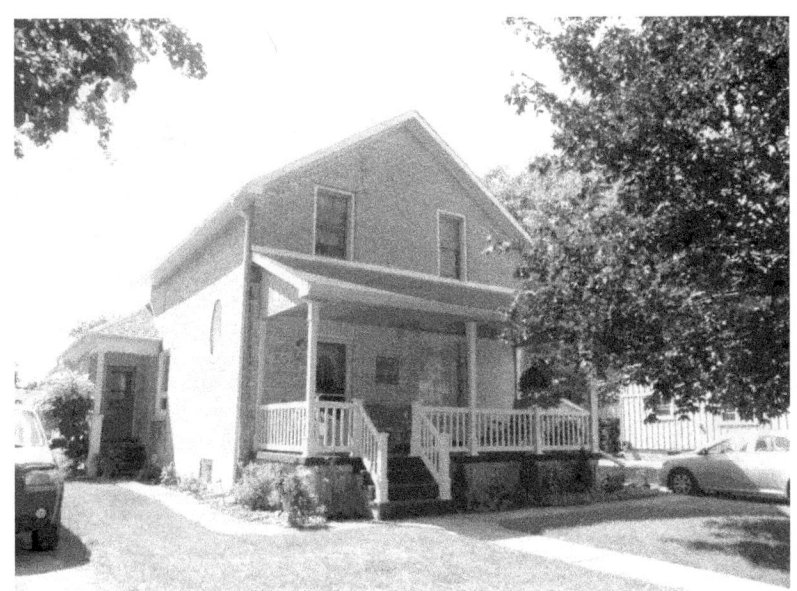

#55 – yellow brick, two storey

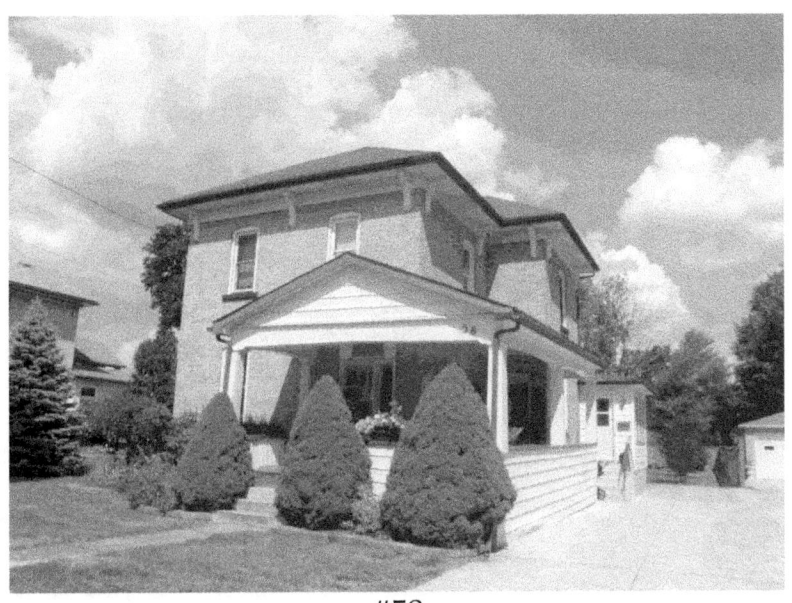

#58

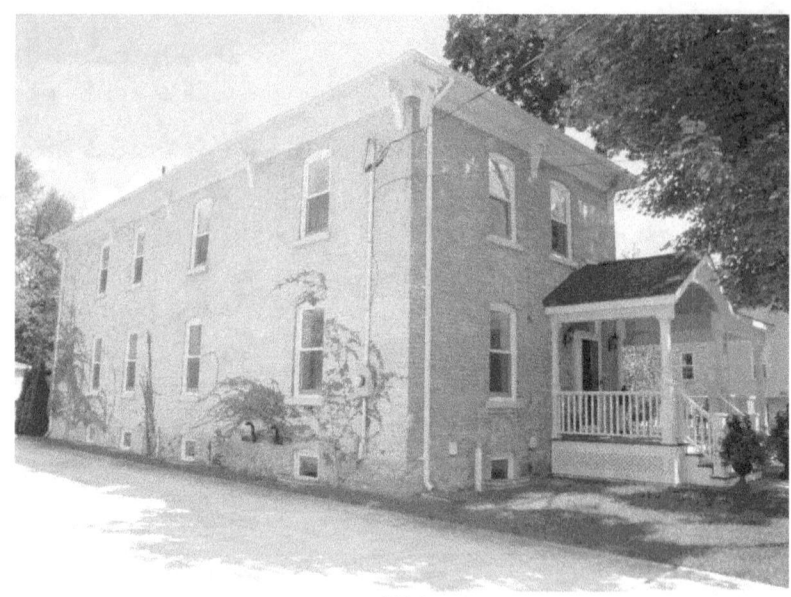

#54

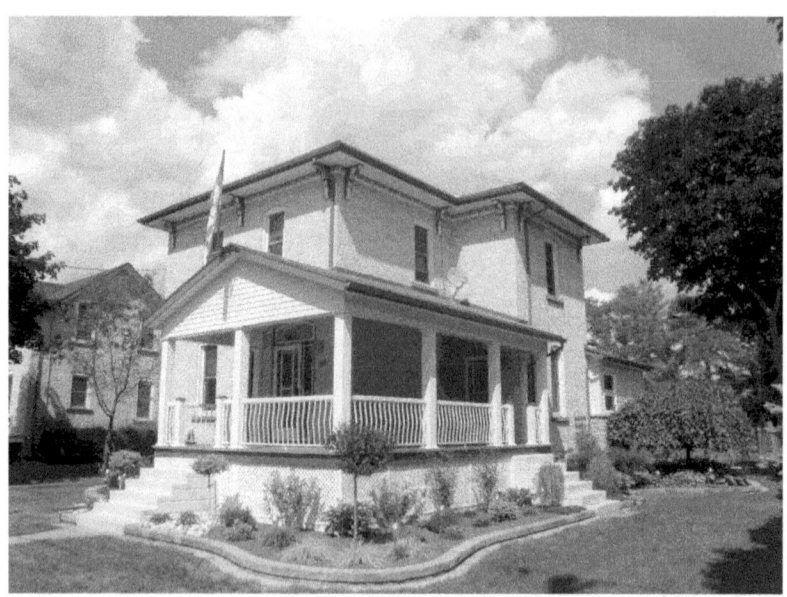

#68 – yellow brick

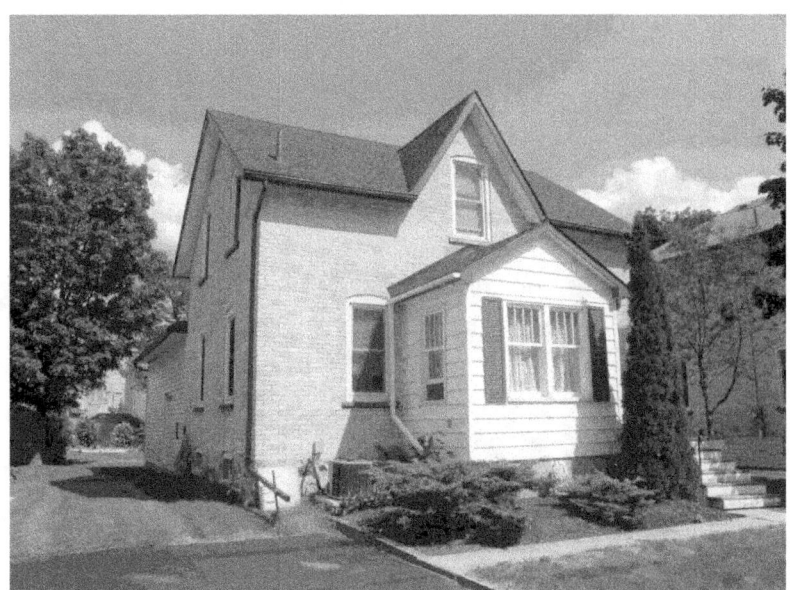

#74 - Yellow brick

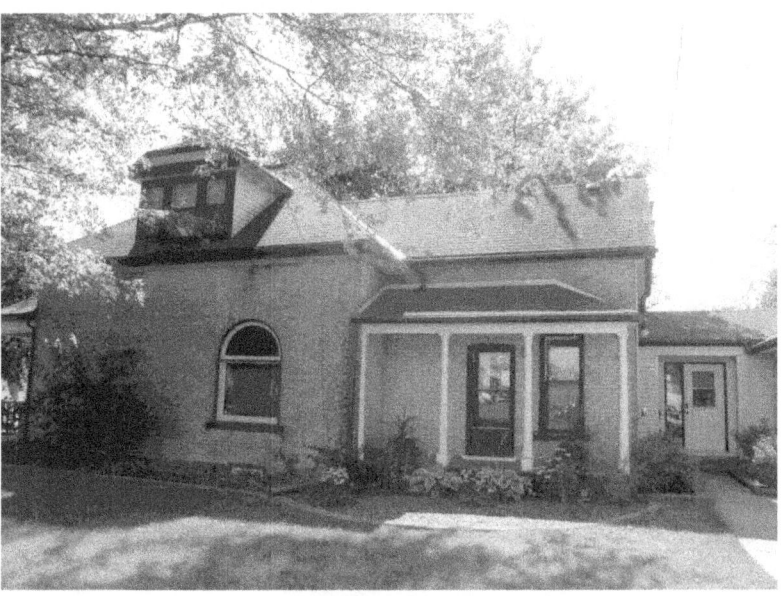

Yellow brick

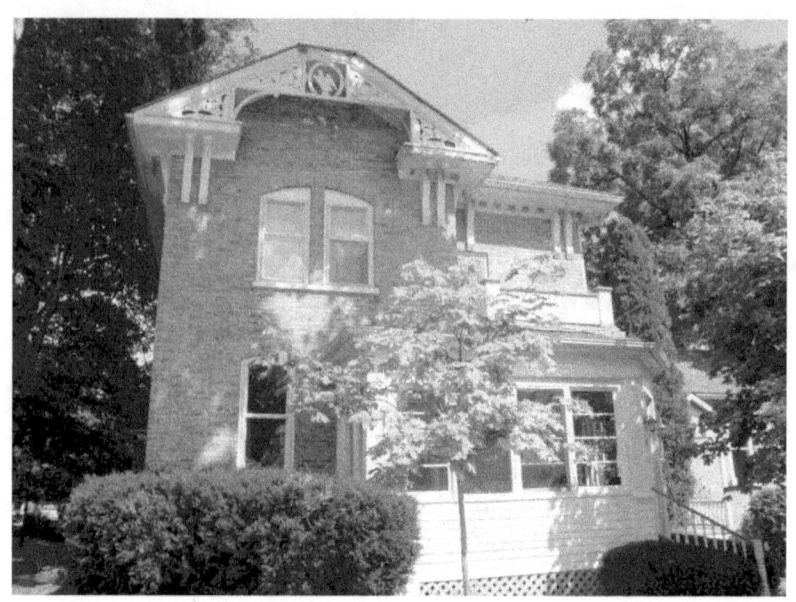

Yellow brick, two storey

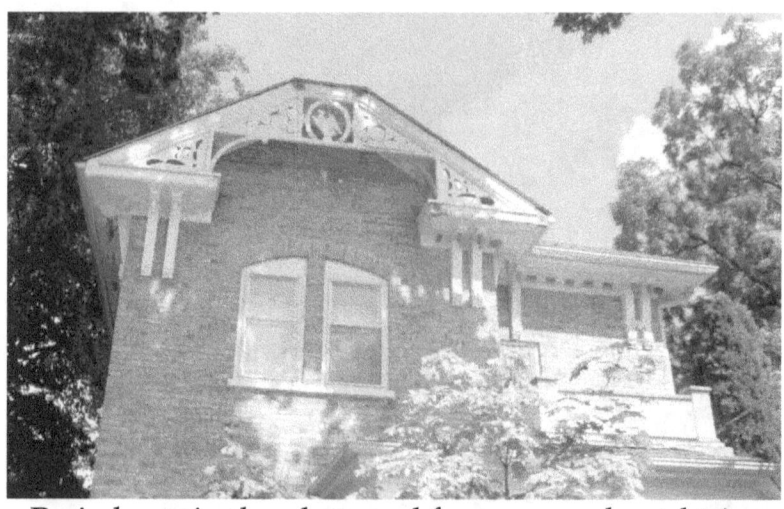

Paried cornice brackets and fancy verge board trim

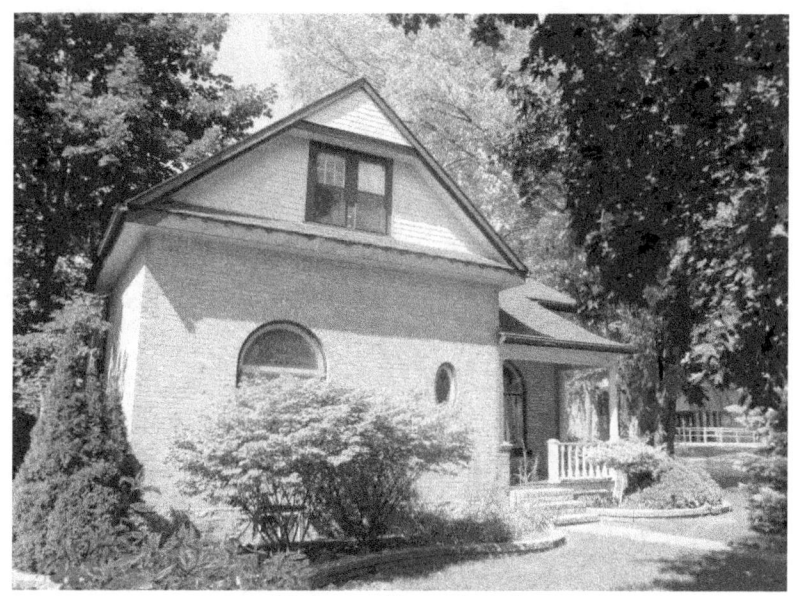

#94 – yellow brick

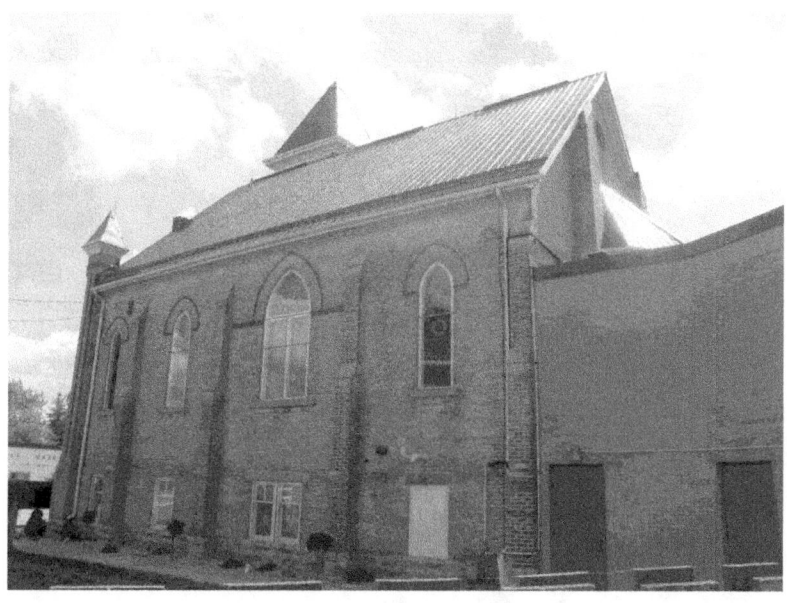

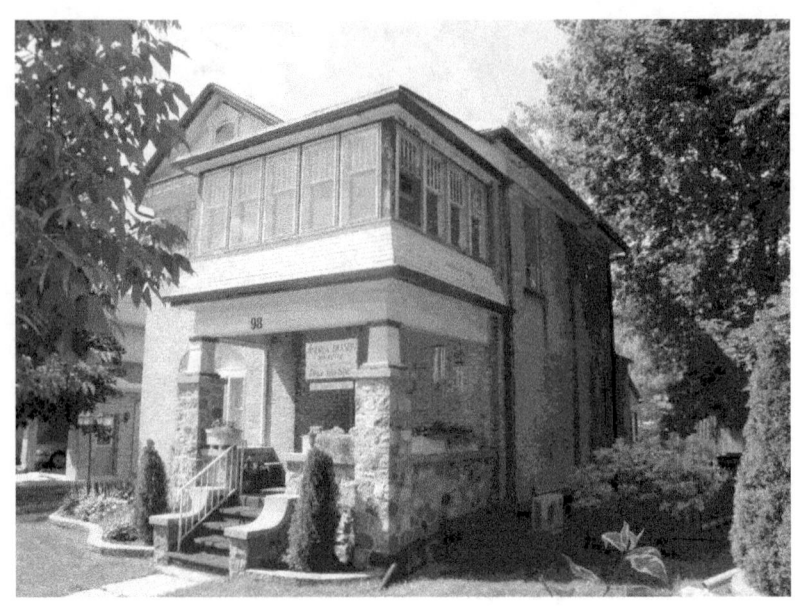

#98

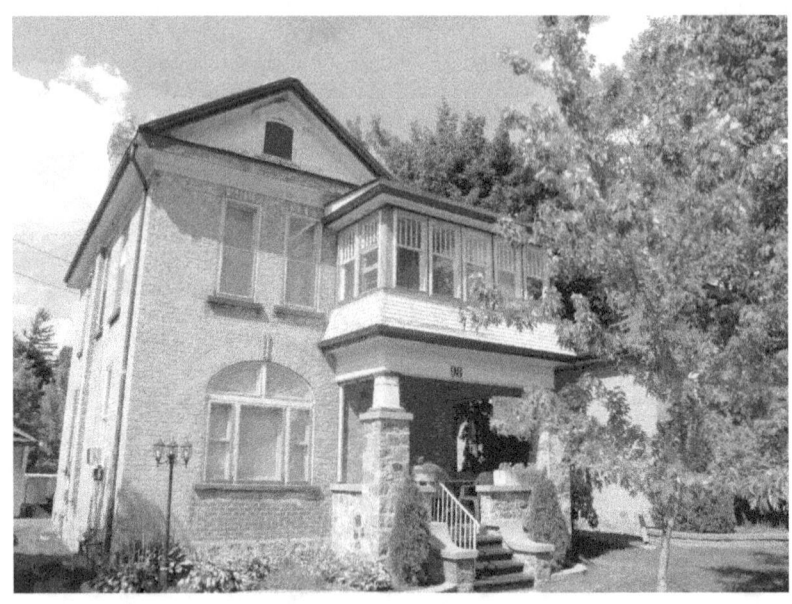

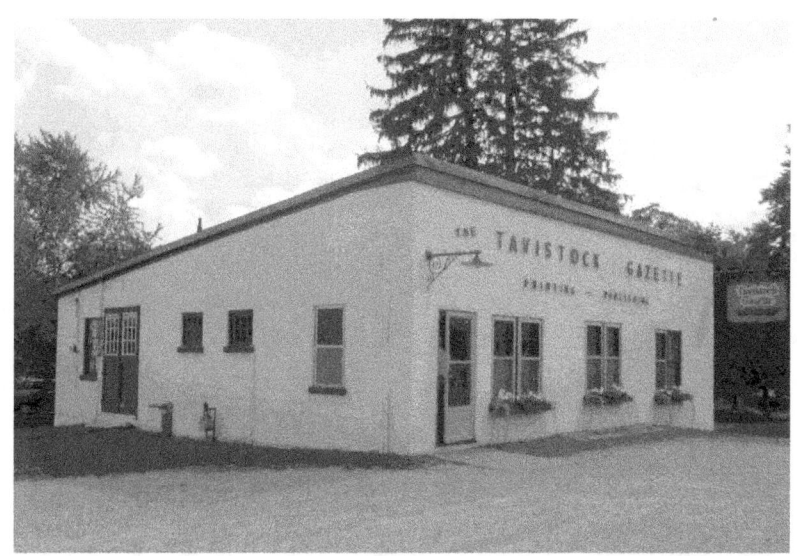

Tavistock Gazette

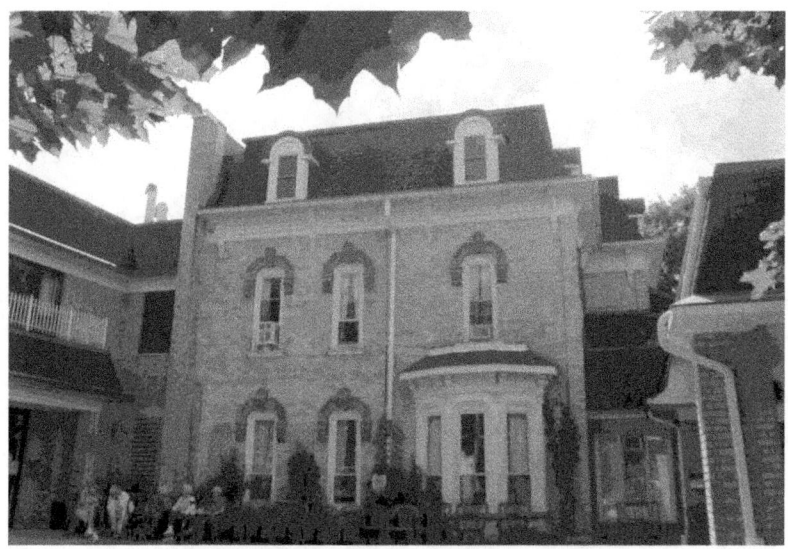

The Maples Home for Seniors
94 William Street

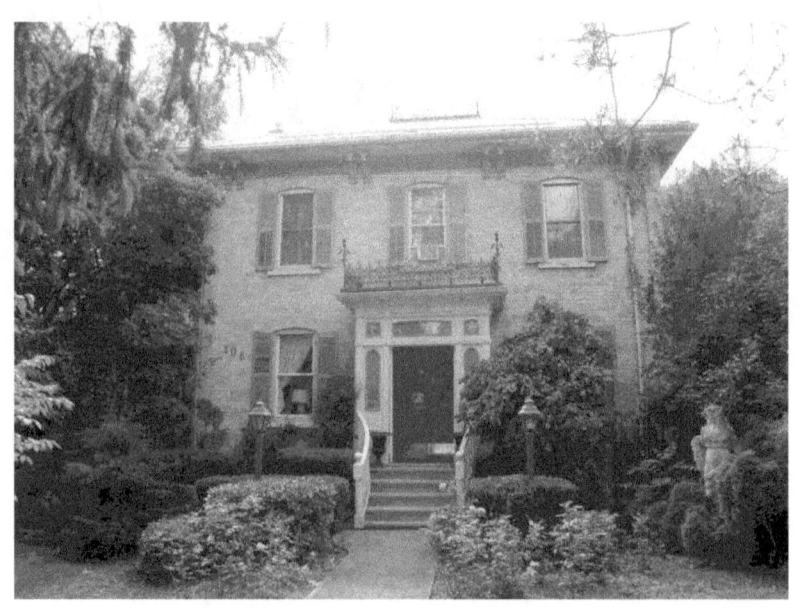

#106 – Georgian style

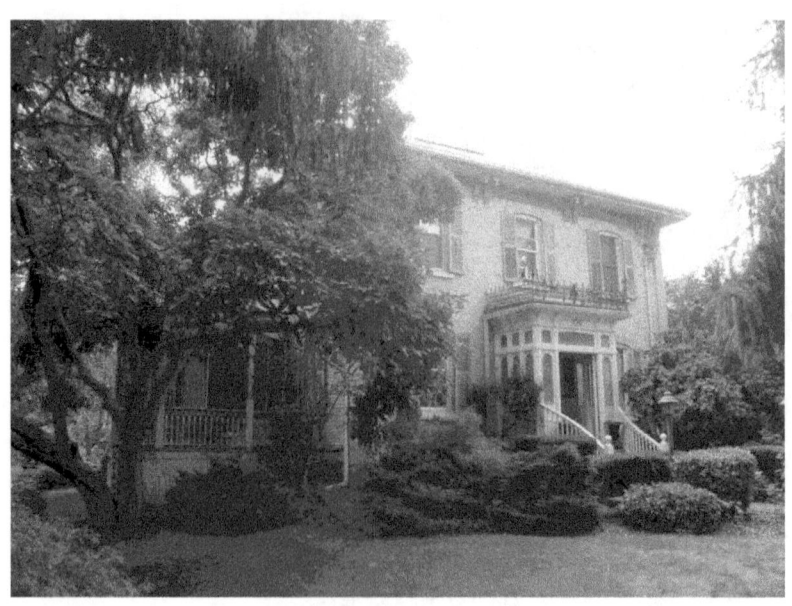

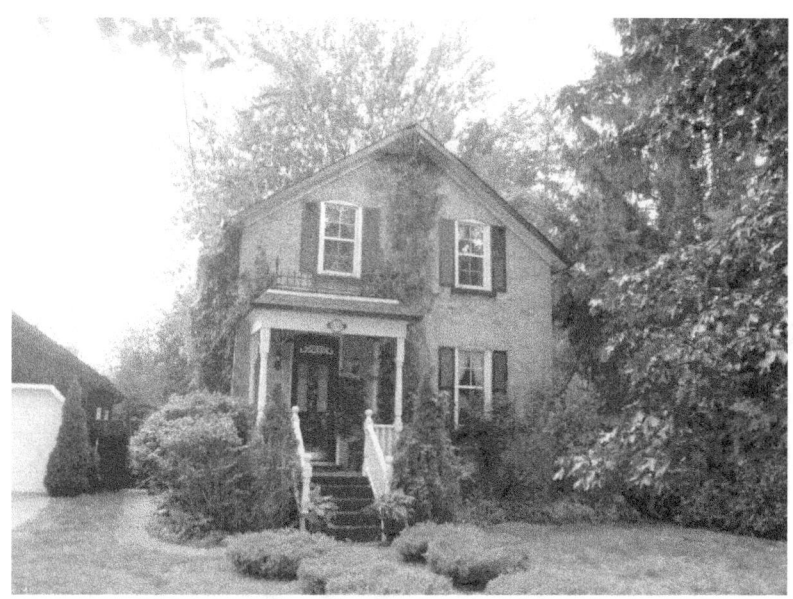

#116 – yellow brick, gingerbread trim

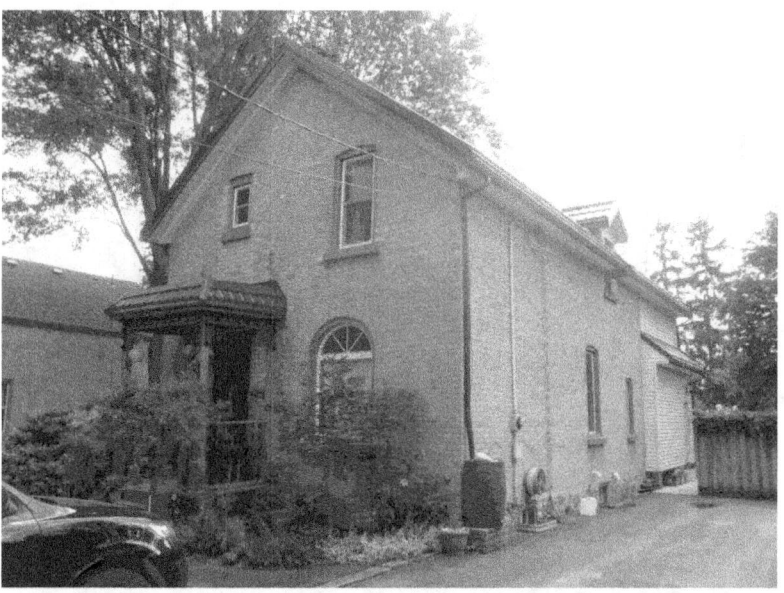

Yellow brick, two storey, dormer window on side

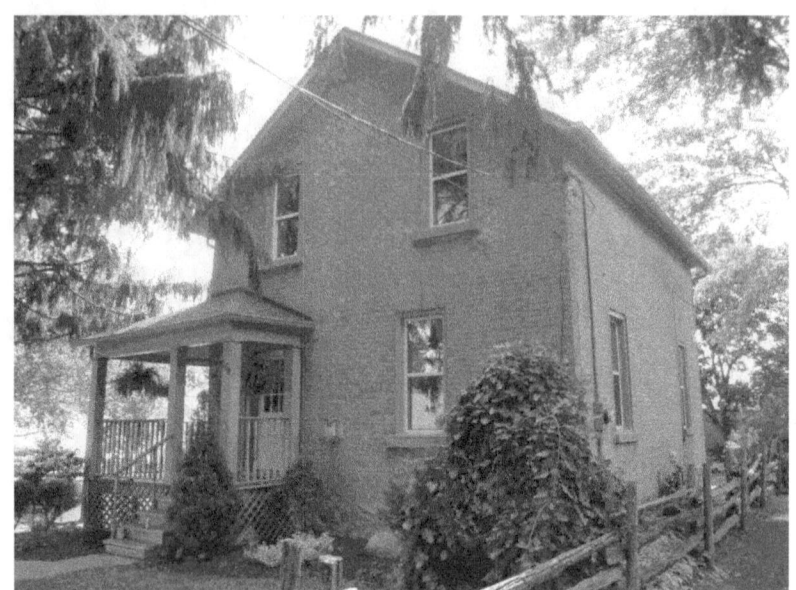

#128 – yellow brick

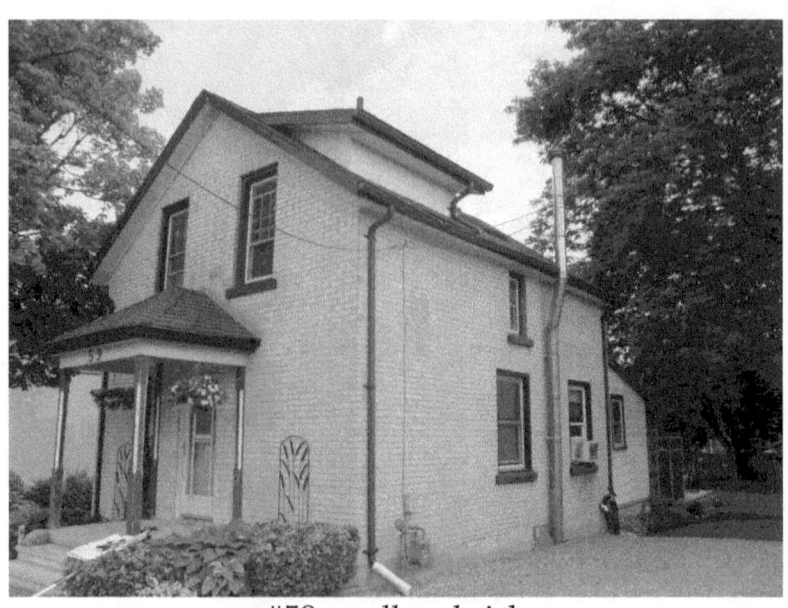

#59 – yellow brick

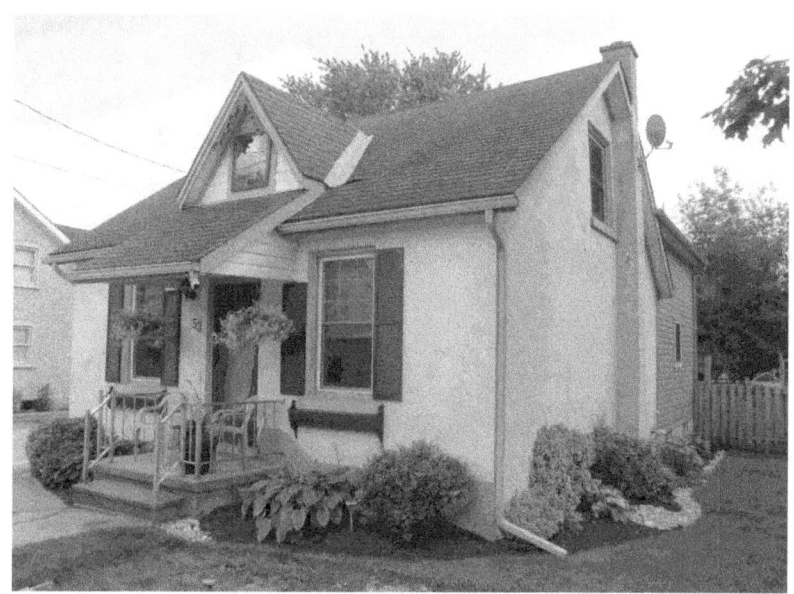

#53 – Gothic Revival cottage

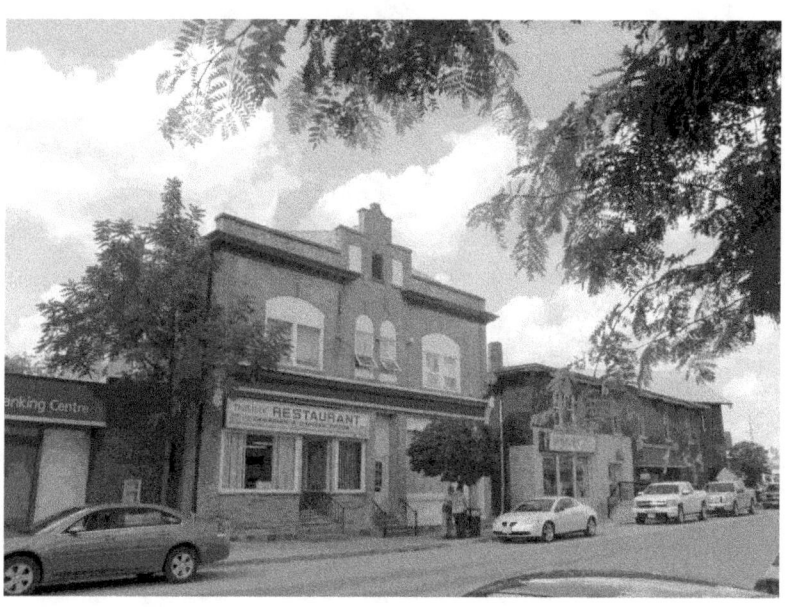

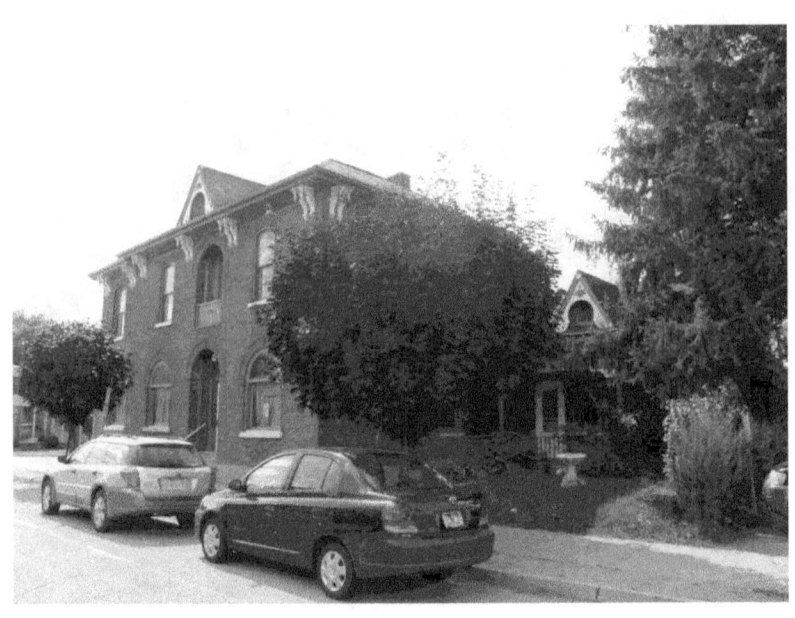

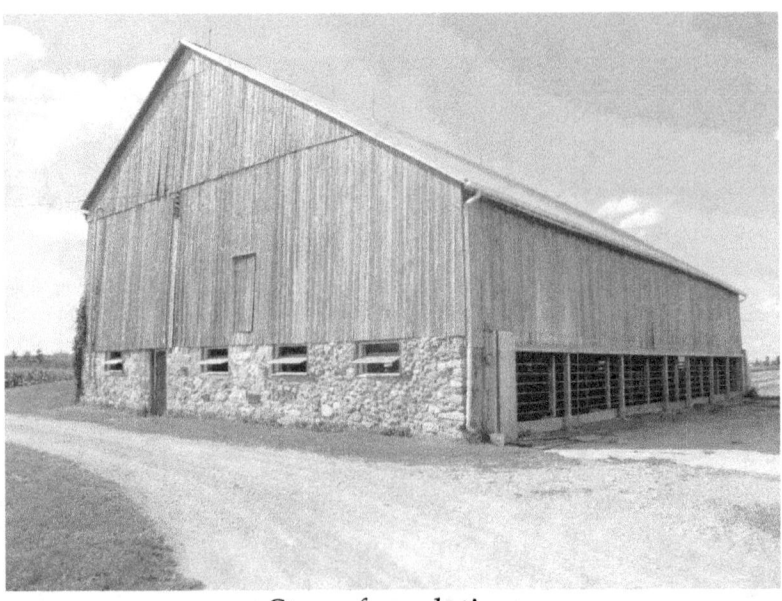

Stone foundation

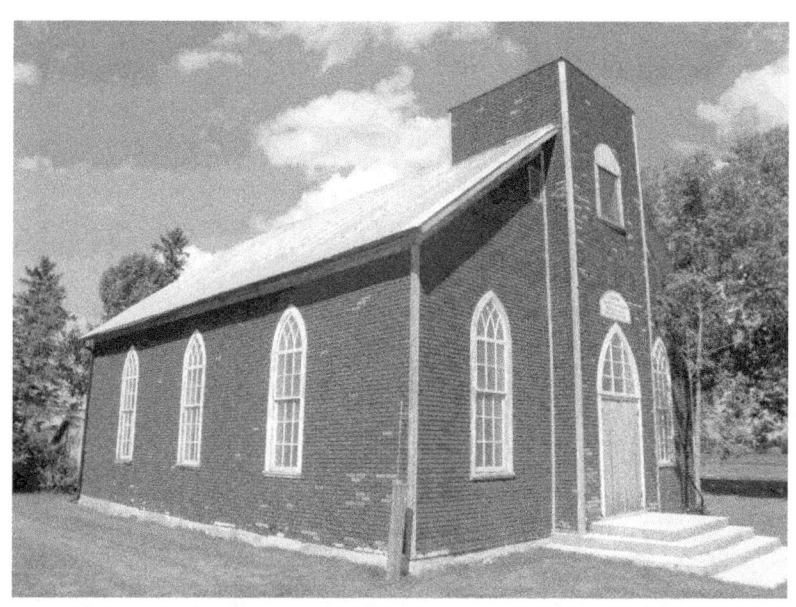

South East Hope Evangelical United - 1874

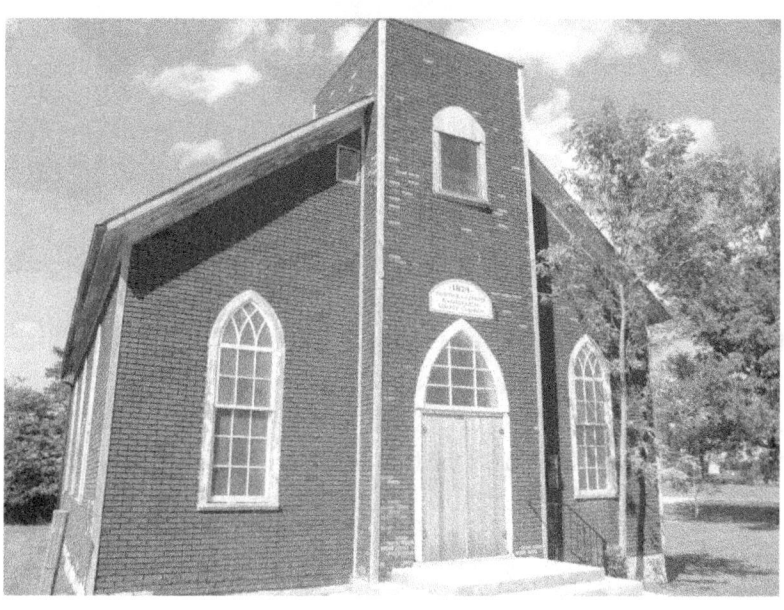

# Baden

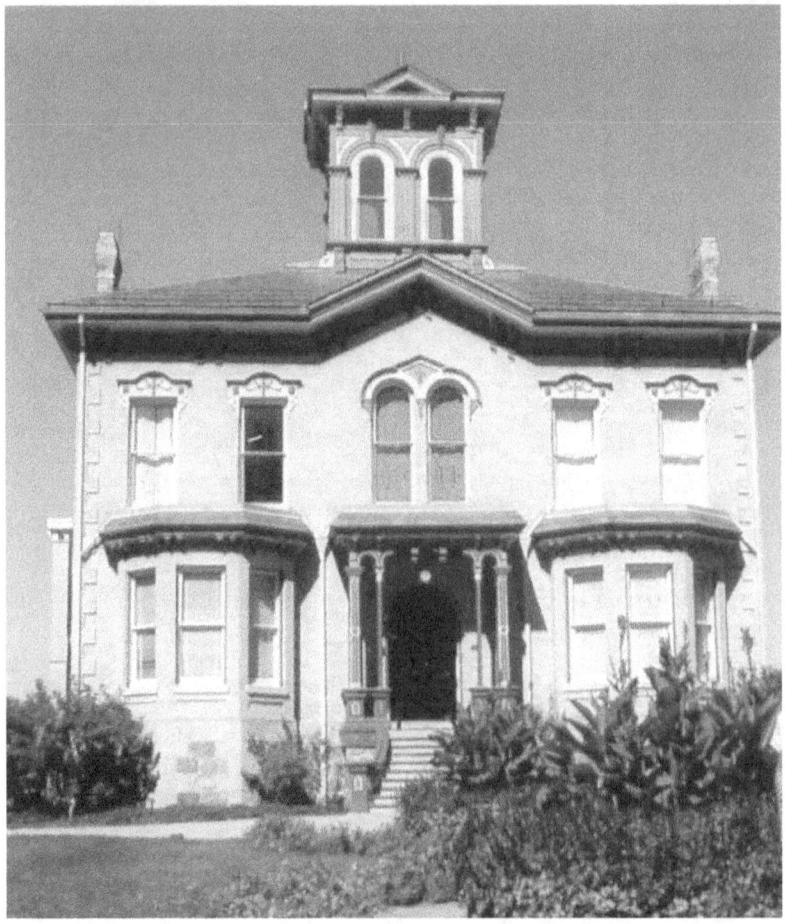

Castle Kilbride is the former residence of James Livingston, a Canadian Member of Parliament and owner of flax and linseed oil mills. It was built in Baden, Ontario in 1877 and named after Livingston's birthplace in Scotland. The major feature of the Castle Kilbride is the interior decorative murals in the style of the Italian Renaissance. The trompe l'oeil technique used in the murals gives the illusion of a third dimension.

# New Hamburg

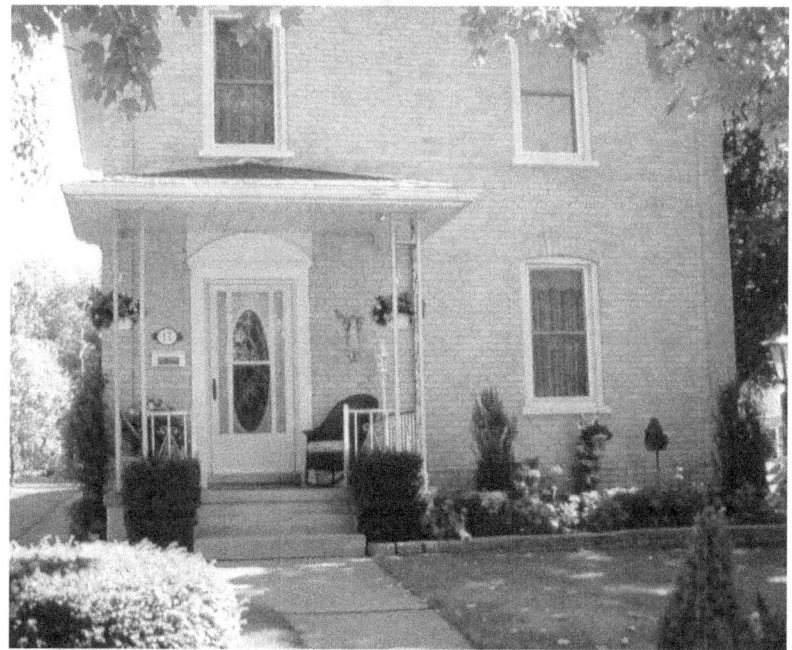

#17 – yellow brick

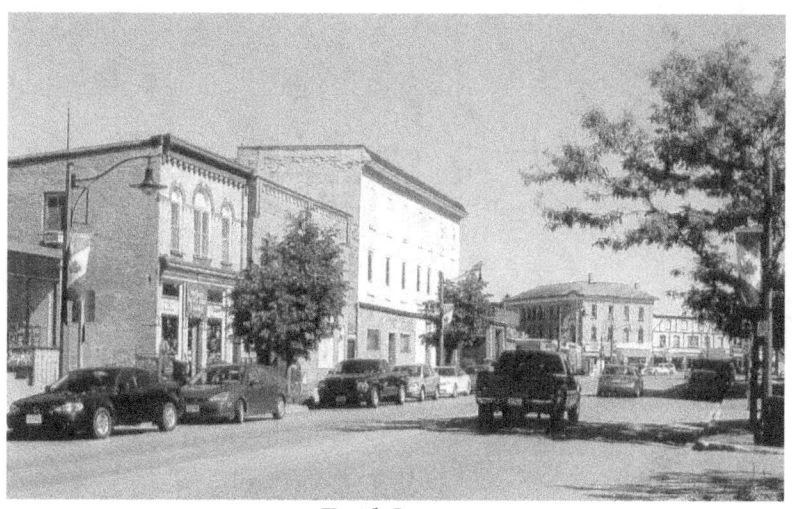

Peel Street

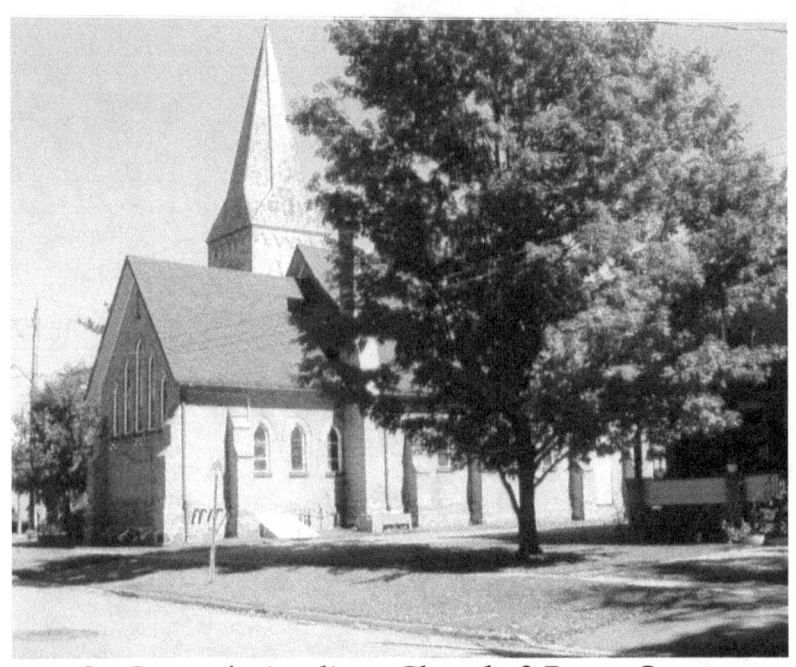

St. George's Anglican Church, 3 Byron Street
– established 1838

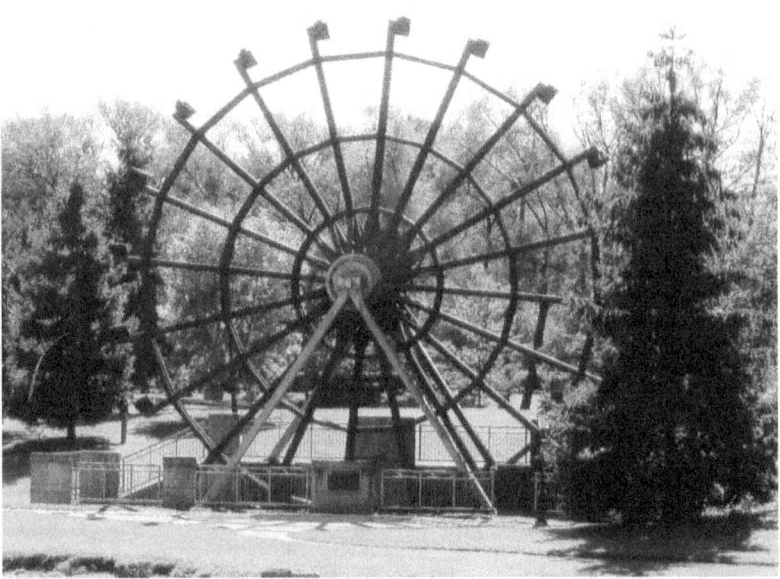

The Heritage Waterwheel is the centrepiece in the riverbank
park system.

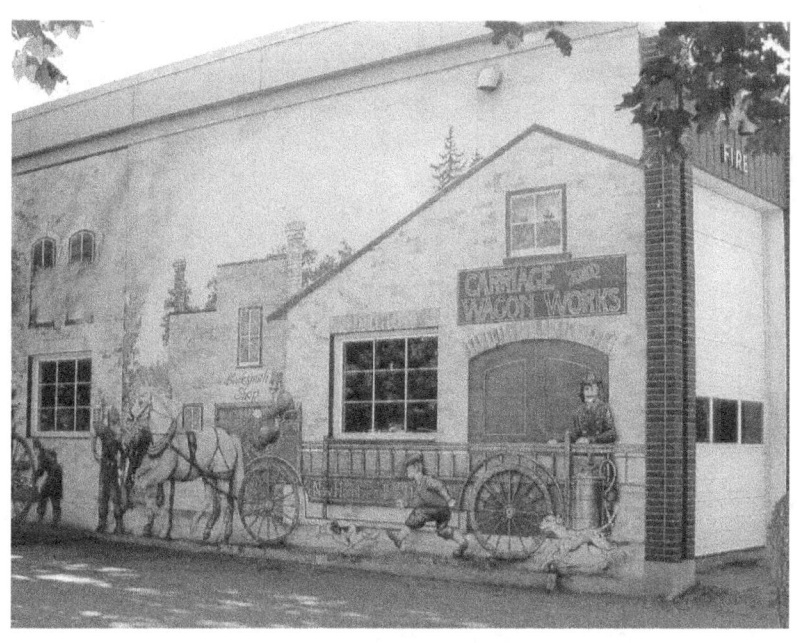

Wall murals

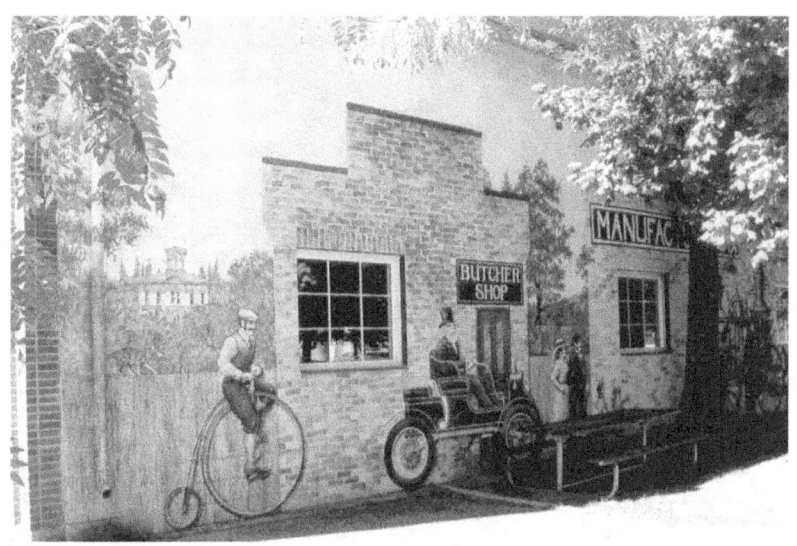

www.ingramcontent.com/pod-product-compliance
Lightning Source LLC
Chambersburg PA
CBHW051305170526
45165CB00004B/1855